lore

T0308927

lore

Davis McCombs

THE AGHA SHAHID ALI PRIZE IN POETRY

THE UNIVERSITY OF UTAH PRESS | *Salt Lake City*

AGHA SHAHID ALI

PRIZE IN POETRY

THE AGHA SHAHID ALI PRIZE IN POETRY

Series editor: Katherine Coles   Advisory editor: Paisley Rekdal

The Defiance House Man colophon is a registered trademark
of the University of Utah Press. It is based on a four-foot-tall
Ancient Puebloan pictograph (late PIII) near Glen Canyon, Utah.

20 19 18 17 16   1 2 3 4 5

LIBRARY OF CONGRESS CATALOGING-IN-PUBLICATION DATA
Name: McCombs, Davis, 1969– author.
Title: lore / Davis McCombs.
Description: Salt Lake City : University of Utah Press, [2016] |
Series: Agha Shahid Ali Prize in Poetry
Identifiers: LCCN 2016006682
ISBN 9781607814818 (paper : alk. paper) | ISBN 9781607814825 (ebook)
Subjects: | BISAC: POETRY / General.
Classification: LCC PS3563.C34348 A6 2016 | DDC 811/.54—dc23
LC record available at http://lccn.loc.gov/2016006682

Printed and bound by Sheridan Books, Inc., Ann Arbor, Michigan.

For Carolyn

contents

foreword

The setting of this extraordinary book is the Ozarks: scrub, fescue, gravel dust, dumpsters, no one's "pastoral dream," especially in winter. Yet, as Davis McCombs writes,

> There's
> something here, isn't there?
> This slope, these old erosions—
> something that isn't a remnant
> of anything.

In thirty-eight haunting poems, McCombs offers that something to us—a wholeness attained not only through the stories and traditions of a culture but also through the fusion of poet and place, poet and past.

During my many readings of *lore*, I watched this fusion take place within and across each of the book's three sections, sometimes dramatically, sometimes quite subtly, as in the poem "Road Trip." Imagine a journey in a small car, its shadow moving across a landscape of "singed and brittle roadside stalks," of "cotton, corn and stubble." As the small shadow progresses, place continues to preside, its oil rig, its burned field "where a windmill / cranks its pinch of rust." Then, in the poem's penultimate stanza,

> We scurry like a flea across the hide of something
> both immense and underfed,
> a creature from the mind's culvert.

As description yields to the poem's central analogy, as the land—and, obliquely, the poem—is seen to be something "both immense and underfed," it is also seen as an act of the mind. In the space of an indented line, McCombs has accomplished a subtle yet sweeping fusion: the fusion of place and imagination that is a prerequisite for lore itself, "creature from the mind's culvert."

It's an insight achieved with masterful economy, an economy shared by many of the book's poems. But a triumph of this collection is its refusal to allow its poems to be held to one method, one means. McCombs is as comfortable with the lyric as he is with the narrative, the riddle, the resolution. And it's through those forms and more that we encounter the widows and children and workers of the Ozarks, the caves and petroglyphs, the animals of legend and the animals of the field. Here are Doc Proffitt, Reid Ramsey, Mac and Barb and Merce. Here is the memory-filled widow in "First Hard Freeze" as she carefully turns a tap to keep the water from freezing—the spout itself a small culvert linking the world of water to the world of the imagination, of dreams:

> On a night like this,
> and in thoughts like these, she is not alone.

The compost hoards its clump of heat; frost
welds the chain to the gate, throwing sparks.
She will lie down to dreams that scatter ahead of her
like snow, but not before she turns the tap one turn,
a hammered metal *drip drip drip* she'll wake to
when a hand not made of hand tests the latch.

A risk in summarizing any work of art is categorization. *Lore*
is not an anthology of ghost stories. It is not a register of eccentric
characters. It isn't an assemblage of remnants, but the creation of
an immensely talented poet who can, with praise, humor, and
sorrow, document a time "between *now here* and *nowhere*," who
can, in short, fuse the gap.

The rewards of this collection are many, but for me its
unwavering precision is the hallmark of McCombs's achievement,
descriptive, figurative, tonal, emotional: all of poetry's rooms are
lit by his lyric accuracy. "To live in the Ozarks," he writes,

is to wait until
the sockets in the bark cry out for eyes.
It is to be ready. Will you set a gourd bowl
brimming shadow at the edge of the coals?

That is precisely what Davis McCombs has done—set before
us a stunning book, brimming shadow, lit by a steady light.

—*Linda Bierds*

lore

Tradition Bearer

Folklore can be collected from almost anyone, but certain people, by virtue of their good memories, long lives, performance skills, or particular roles within a community, are often especially well qualified to provide information. Folklorists sometimes refer to these people as "tradition bearers."

—"Conducting Fieldwork," The American Folklife Center

First Hard Freeze

The first hard freeze, an owl beyond the twig
at the window like the shadow of a thought
across the mask of a face, and whatever it is
that will unmask the girl who masks the old
woman who is turning the tap comes crawling
up from timber on a night like this, comes
wandering like wind when everything else
is frosty and still: the deer, unbuckled, the field
a matted bulge, and the flashlight's beam
that will not come to light the fires of their eyes.
On a night like this, the old woman will think
secretly of the dead in their graves, of satin
and of wood and of a dark that pours itself
into a vessel it will never fill. On a night like this,
and in thoughts like these, she is not alone.
The compost hoards its clump of heat; frost
welds the chain to the gate, throwing sparks.
She will lie down to dreams that scatter ahead of her
like snow, but not before she turns the tap one turn,
a hammered metal *drip drip drip* she'll wake to
when a hand not made of hand tests the latch.

A Family Story

Mac knew Philpot was his sweetums' other,
but for a month he ran a calloused thumb
along the knife-edge of revenge, and pondered:

how, exactly, to exact it? He thought of emptying
a box of roofing nails where the road veered off
to Piss-pot's lonely house. (He'd taken

to noodling with the name's unkindest variants.)
He thought of lighting a gas-can with a wick
and lobbing it into Pot-head's hayloft.

No, not right. He dithered, brooded, stalled...
but happenstance would choose The Watering Hole—
night of the mechanical bull, a draft-beer twofer special.

Outside the honky-tonk, a feckless wind blundered
up Futz Creek, moonsplay cold on the shallows,
but inside, the trapped heat was roaring to a kiln.

Fuck's yore prob? Mac spat, and the throng
went pin-drop. The two grappled, a shot's report...
Pill-pop lurched from the scene, a bullet in his shin;

Mac strutting toward the not-so-distant night
he'd wrap his Trans around a light pole and sustain
an identical limp, a karmic twinning that did not

cool the blood between them—or so I've been told.

Wind in the Ozarks

It files and defiles.
It pounds at the door in the dead of night.
It plays odd chords on the shed's warped slats.
It cries like a child in an upstairs crib.
It scurries and scratches in the wall.
It whines. It flakes the paint.
It curls the roof's tin edge.
It peels the snow in tendrils off the bluff.
It loosens a crack in the rock, worrying it like a tooth.
It is a mallet, a sledge.
It dents and chisels.
It scuffs the pond's clear lens.
It whips the bungied, flapping tarp off the woodpile
and lets the rain soak in.
It seeks the hearth where the damp logs hiss and pop,
and drifts like a spirit down the flue.
It moans the embers' long collapsing sigh.
It frays the curtain. It tatters the web.
It scours the glass with a flung fistful of grit.
It rips and tears. It jimmies the catch.
It pries the window with a blade like a knife.
It covers the tracks of the thief.

It rattles. It batters.
It seeps and ekes.
It finds the candle in a shuttered room
and slants the wax across the nub.
It whistles. It hums. It baits
the moon's brass hook with a cloud
and trolls the hills
for the dark that will swallow us whole.

Dumpster Honey

The bees were working the contents
of the fenced-in metal trash bin,
zigging and scribbling past the goo

of candy wrappers and the sticky rims
of dented cans, entering, as they might
a blossom, the ketchup-smeared burger

boxes and the mold-fuzzed, half-eaten
fruity snack packs, those food-grade waxes
mingling with Band-Aids and a limp

"We're #1" foam finger while on top
of the disposable wet mop redolent of solvents
and fresheners, the F.D.&C. Red No. 40

nontoxic food pigment leaked
from a bloated dip packet where the bees
were buzzing and collecting the high-fructose

corn nectars of that uncompacted jumble
and returning, smudged with the dust
of industrial pollens, to, perhaps, some

rusted tailpipe hive where their queen
grew fat on the froth of artificial sweeteners
out back of the little oily gas station

in the middle of Arkansas where we pulled off
to change the baby's diaper and had to ask
for the key they kept on a giant ring.

In His Own Country

Old Doc Proffitt plunged into the wind outside the quonset's off-plumb lintel,
    a blast that slapped at him like wet burlap. It was two a.m.: another child
        yanked howling into these stone hills, and now he pushed
            into the lashing rain and toward his Chevy wagon hulking

as if tethered to the shuddering catalpa. He'd have to hurry now
    or the low beam bridge that yawned between him and the quilted bier
        of his own bed might be out: Ah, spring in the Ozarks:
            that strobed, heart-battering fist of a season.

He fought the wheel, the heavy lure of sleep, the wiper blades sluicing ropes
    of water off the glass, and by the time he made the turn where the road
        dropped down to the level of the creek, the radials were spewing
            mud, and then the bridge appeared, its guardrail swimming

into the headlights where a figure clad in oilskin slumped. He didn't know how
    he knew; he just did—not a whiff of brimstone, the horns hidden
        by the drooping fedora off which the raindrops poured in veils:
            Sumbitch settin' there, Doc said, *like he owned that country.*

Long story short, he did, but Old Doc helped the Devil out that night,
    the way he told it, extracting an abscessed molar with the puller from his bag—
        a deal, once struck, that bought the people of that place a pause
            before the fires of damnation, a chance.

Don't you see? Doc would tell them. *There's still time to set things right.*
    He kept that tooth, an evil-looking spike, in a drawer of his roll top desk
        and, if asked, would produce it for the deeply skeptical parade
            of hillfolk through his office.

Goddamn rock, looked to me like, one was heard saying as he limped
    from the waiting room on crutches and turned back toward the hills,
        that rough and tumbled country damned, no doubt, by God.

Freshwater Drum

In certain parts of Kentucky's cave country it is possible to drop a
buoyant object in a sinkhole and then retrieve it, often hours later,
when it floats up in a bluehole spring. A watermelon, for instance,
after having traveled the length of some underground stream,
emerges chilled to a cool 54 degrees.

Once there was a boy; and once, the sun a tarnished silver plate
   between the pole bean vines, he led her under barbed wire
and down a ditch to a tar-black smear that gave back nothing
   but their own hearts pumping. This is a song of gravel dust
and fescue, of balance won, and a metal culvert's stagnant slubs.
   This is a music of the heart's solidity. He showed her how
to thump the rind, their faces shadowed on its lightning stripes.
   He showed her how a shirt, untucked, can make a basket
for lugging a burden down a red clay wash. Sixty years, the sun
   still askew above the hill, and now she carries only the song,
but the boy is inside it, and the melon, too, and when she follows
   its sequence of familiar notes along that weedless rut
she finds two bicycles propped at the head of a path angling
   down mud and hoofprints to a knob of water blossoming
and blossoming, she finds the white perch drumming its tendons

by the undercut silt bank, finds the stream's clear discharge,
how it nudged the river's muddle, and they waited, the cold interior
    of that music she would not yet hum nor carry, coming numbly
among facets. She follows the song where it leads: past
    the striped and oblate orb that wavered into focus there
below the ledge, over the black seeds in a half-moon on the sand,
    and to the grave in which, come that winter, the boy would lie.

Gray Fox, a Resolution of Sorrow

WHEREAS, the fox would stand still blinking at the swingset's blur among the leaves and ratcheting of chains and how by this we knew that she had mastered something of the twitch that deeply gripped her.

WHEREAS, the fox would cross that edge so lately shuddering limbs upon the bass and strobe of storm that she did not, that once, remarkably appear at the accustomed hour, though from the rain-lit panes we watched for her and too were shaken.

WHEREAS, the lithic gloom or chambered stump in which she curled belatedly remained, though very near, unknown to us.

WHEREAS, the fox was seen so recently upon the asphalt twisted dimmed by vultures flapping branchward that we did not at first know her who had by then unraveled down the actual trunks and through the hollow where we slept.

WHEREAS, she was omnivorous and monogamous both and by these traits we recognized her weaving shape

across the slope where broomsedge marked her coat in
grizzled light.

WHEREAS, she was seen that winter once to whirl upon
the night's white crux and sideways glitter flakes into
the cloud through which she spun and passed our
flashlit grasp.

WHEREAS, three kits at last confirmed the summer's
wax, their black-tipped tails still dripping from the
glaciated span in which their kind had first appeared
and then dispersed.

NOW THEREFORE BE IT HERE RESOLVED that we
express our appreciation and our sorrow.

FURTHERMORE, be it directed that this resolution shall
be spread upon the minutes of that hour between *now
here* and *nowhere* and the meeting of the creek's blue
flank where, by her prints, she was known to pass, and
that a copy of same shall be provided to the wind.

The Widder Mercer

I'm holed up in the greenhouse sowing flats of buttercrunch
    when she arrives,
a ghost from the wild winter light outside the polycarbonate,
    her hair disheveled
from the frantic wind—just as it must have been the night
    old Merce fell
off the chimney and she walked the four miles to the nearest house,
    Reid Ramsey's,
who followed her, back along the path where her footprints,
    small as hooves,
and the cane's insistent period were still visible in the snow—
    or so they said.
She was ancient even then; impossible to think she'd still be there,
    scratching at the hard earth
out back of the leaning barn that even thirty years ago a swath
    of trumpet vine
was pulling to the ground. Impossible, but then I'm in the truck
    bouncing over chip
and gravel and down into the holler they still call Waverly's—
    her people, not his.
They brought the backhoe up and over her flowerbeds and dropped

Merce's coffin

in a man-sized ditch just shy of the porch where he'd been apt to sit
        of an evening

sucking tar into his lungs and cussing Ramsey under his breath—
        so I know

he's still there, but what of the stable, the coop, the buckets of grain,
        and that smell

of woodsmoke and ham that would hit you when you'd open
        the door? Are they?

I will say this: 1) Crows that believe themselves unobserved
        will make the oddest,

almost human noises in their corvid throats. 2) The wind
        that brought her

blew the glowing cedars out all across that little valley. 3)
        Branches rose

in the headlights and turned away, scraping their antlers on the glass.

Of Thorns

Go down our potholed road, past the last light in the last house
and the old glass foundry now slated for demolition, go past
the tattered heaps of salted snow, the tracks, a cold sun sliding
like an egg yolk off a plate and over the cross-tied edge
of the world, and you will come to where the creek, in flood,
scrapes a rut through gravel, but it shouldn't be a problem,
not this time of year, and finally the road just peters out
into a deer track and then not even that—just hills, just Arkansas—
and it's not pretty, not anybody's pastoral dream, only scrub
and broken bottles, and that rusted pipe through which,
improbably, a dogwood has found the light, and there's no shepherd
stepping from the trees with his crook, not even the curve of moon
that gathers each night its flock of polished stones, but down there
in that shabby closeness, that's where whatever it is that saves me is,
where, praise be to something, it waits in briars like Jesus or literature.

Trundle

I dream so often now across this vast plateau, the broken dome
    of granite... I've come to call the Ozarks home.
        Some nights I find the bent shape of the great bull

brooding starrily over our field, the sky turning like spokes
    above a herd of winter-thinning deer who fold up,
        with frost on their ribs, to sleep, and I think of people

I never knew: there's Maw Earl on a straw mattress fighting to bring
    her seventh, and final, child into these hills—a boy at last,
        after six little girls. And there's the father, old Satch,

staggering around the barn with a Mason jar half-full of the liquid
    that will drown him, and praying *sweet-and-merciful-Savior-*
        oh-please for a son. And there's little Kit at the foot

of her trundle, about to be supplanted; she's saying her own prayer
    that the baby, christened Azariah, but known as Scuppernong,
        Oh-Jesus-can-you-hear-me-I'll-do-anything, will die.

He doesn't, and ten years later, more or less, he'll be cleaning a shotgun...
    It's so easy now to see the burnished light in the orchard,
        the yellow jackets heckling the windfall apples, Maw

on the porch shelling beans; I can hear the pings they make
    against the pan, and then the explosion. No doctor near,
        and not a dime to their names, his foot will never heal,

not properly, and so it's Scup now, who knocks once at my office door
    and enters as the last orange glow retracts across the boxwood
        out the window—*Gonna be a cold one, Professor*—

and hobbles in with his four-legged cane to empty my small trash can
    into a larger one with wheels.

Liquid Assets

In time, you'll come to see the pond's scuffed monocle
under a cloud-tossed Texas sky, a goldfinch twitching
from the tree line. Couple of drinks—it doesn't take much—
and Barb will edge the conversation toward the precipice
that is the land she owns and is planning to go back to;
you'll learn it's half a farm—her split of a divorce settlement.
You'll come to imagine the NO TRESPASSING signs tacked
along the access road, old Whatshisface, her ex, stalking
his side of the wire, still sucking on a flint-sharp grudge.
There's a barn there too, or was, last time she checked,
its window snagging the sun that sinks into the hill.
She says she's ordering some pines to dibble-in along
the boundary when she gets down there next, that's the plan,
going to build a little cabin eventually. She's gesturing.
She sees it all: a brood of chicks under a heat lamp,
an ungulate or two, who knows? She's shaping the basin
of the spring, miming how she'll scoop it out, the dripping
of its liquid like the ticking of a clock whose hands
have led her round and round that hill: the redbud's blotch
along the rise, the slope, the shed, the rusted nail on which
she'll hang that grass-stained scythe that is the moon.

Deterred

And so I came to be the man who hunched
at the desk under the lamp for six blind months
and followed the loops of cursive spiraling
backward like the song of a wood thrush
to the creek below the hermit's ink-black cave
and the knob of water at its source braiding
and unbraiding down rock shelves opening
a crease into the stone of the hill. One night
a storm thrashed the house, but I did not look up
at the sound of rain's hard fist against the pane,
or thunder kicking in a door. I was standing
in the leafiest, greenest light, the stream beside me
tumbling as it would unceasing from the nib
so dazzlingly, so sparklingly... no. And that
was when I knew he'd heard it: a brittle sound
like a dry leaf flipped by wind (a page turning),
that was when I knew that he was clawing up
through mud, rising strobed and tattered,
and that soon I'd feel his boot steps on the porch,
his hand reaching out, reaching for the screen door's
latch that, grasped, became the pen I lifted.

Sight Unseen

It's past crepuscular when I pull up to the old pipe gate
and park, a fine snow glittering like stubble in the beams.
I'm waiting, waiting... but for what? The man I'm named for
bought this place without ever having set foot on it.
I'm older now than he was then, too old to be brooding
over phantoms, but like it or not, I'm hitched, as he was,
to this 200-acre plow, following a furrow that keeps
circling back and back. I was here forty years ago, a child
in the cab of his truck: another winter dusk, a pencil nub
in the glove compartment, the smell of corncobs—
and out of that pitchless dark: cattle, smoke-breathed, jostling,
this side of the fence, the *wrong* side; by then I'm whimpering.
Hush now. A bent T-post. *They won't hurt you.* Pliers, staples.
You just think they will. And then he's out beyond the idling
headlights' reach, following a line of metal thorns. Does he
make his way back here too? I don't know. But I'm here, for now:
the smell of the heater the same, the dark's unaltered vigil,
my old fear exactly what it was: that I'll never see him again.

Found Downriver

Take Chittsburg, or what we dubbed it
(you get one guess): po-dunk, provincial—

just like home—but come the dregs
of Saturday's truck pull or barn dance,

every drunk in West Kentucky would
start dreaming of the old truss bridge

over the clanking current that drained
the hills of our dry counties and marked

the boundary between Pentecostal and Papist.
These were our neighbors, our teachers, lost

behind the wheels of Broncos and Cutlasses
that swam the weaving back roads toward

the neon lure of DK's Roadhouse, just across
the line, and Chittsburg, that bend in the asphalt

where garden gnomes gave way to concrete
Virgin Marys. From the gravel parking lot

just off the square, we kids would race
each other to Terry's Tapes & Threads,

a beaded lair of mildew, vinyl, and silk-
screen T-shirts where we'd hang out and where,

behind the mirrored counter, Terry himself,
the subject of rumors (What sort of a man

likes to sew?) tried to make a go
of that doomed venture—kind,

indulgent Terry—whispered about, hounded,
until he too was dreaming of that bridge.

Road Trip

Over the singed and brittle roadside stalks,
   over cotton, corn, and stubble,
      our car's dark bug shape slithers.

Over the metal drainpipe, over the oil rig,
   and the burned field where a windmill
      cranks its pinch of rust, we are

a hurried sweep of shadow, a sleek, chromatic gleam
   the cold sun follows
      with its blue-orange dot of concentration.

We scurry like a flea across the hide of something
   both immense and underfed,
      a creature from the mind's culvert,

an animal concocted out of barbed-wire ribs
   and cockleburs, the grass its rippling fur
      through which our small wake passes like a shiver.

Postcard from the Ozarks: Winter

Snow fell like fireflies sprayed with an insecticide.
It was just that swift, that brutal. *Cold, huh?* I ask
my neighbor, who is leaning on a shovel when I trudge past.
Sonsabitchin mailman, he replies. *I'm waitin on
that sonofabitch.* Some nights I watch him burning garbage
in a metal drum; some nights, when the wind's just wrong,
I wade through the river of dioxins and hydrofluoric acids
burbling up the hill to pool around our swingset's insect legs.
You ever smell the label melting off a milk jug? I have.
I peer through the trees while his flop-eared mutt pounds
an ellipse of mud around the barrel's glowing rim,
and I tremble with an anger as naked and as raw as the moon,
but what can I do? For now, I kick on through the still
faintly convulsing drifts to a door that shuts behind me
like a lid. Nights like this, even the knob grows fur.

Reunion

There is a field and inside the field is a broken-down question,
sharp as a barb.

There is a glazed-brick silo and inside the silo is the solution
suggested long ago by a wedding.

There is the shadow of the beloved oak and within the shadow is
the hair of the dead man's lover.

There is the humped haystack and somewhere under it is the
misery that ran between two people like a tilting fence.

There are the shreds of clouds and just beyond them is an
immense and swift and brutal fall.

There is a gravel road and somewhere down it, out of sight, is an
hour of ardent subterfuge.

There is a pond and near its rim, at the verge of starvation, are the
words that have allowed her to go on.

Not Untwist

The fescue stretched to the door of the white farmhouse
and a cold sun hammered planks of light onto the barn
and on a clump of tilted outbuildings. I drove that plunging road
all winter, past the old farm and the boundary fence
where three hogs' heads had been nailed to a board.
They stared with their withering eyes at the road
and the skin shrank away from their teeth and blackened.
I didn't think of them except in those moments, rounding
the turn and coming up over grass, when they were before me.
Wind whined through their ribs of wire and each day
shriveled down to the hill's bitter dark and the block of light
from the window where the old farmer must have sat,
asleep in front of the television. Something about the place
troubled me—if only fitfully and only vaguely. Yes,
something was happening there or about to happen.
It trembled in the dry chickweed under the fence or waited
where the barn strained its wedge of shadow toward the pond.
Once, I saw the old man, thin as a stalk, climbing up into the seat
of an ancient tractor. I didn't wave. I didn't stop and take it in,
and then the morning, pale and warm, the car lifting over
the seedheads, when I saw the grass charred nearly to the fence,
a heap of ash still trickling smoke where the house had stood.

Aubade for the Yazoo Clipper

The story of your life is the story of the dream
you climb the rungs of sleep down into:
a toolshed's oily clutter where Mobley—*I ain't*
seen you since I died—still putters among the grease
and coffee cans of sorted bolts, and it is out
of that mown slumber that this contraption
of blades and pulleys has returned, this mower
for the deep and obsolescent South, and you
have come back on the very day still tinted
by a slosh of gas, the muffler's spark on rainbow,
and Mobley gone in the instant spluttering to smoke
because he thought to save the old Yazoo, to drag it
from the shed that was by then a latticed photo
negative of flame, and the hell of that blaze
is the block of sun through the window you wake to.

The Hill Itself

I walk beside the bluff's occlusion
on a day when spring is shaking
fistfuls of wild onions in the grass.
A pickup rattles over the cattle
grate: one old man looking for
another old man, something
about wanting to buy a model
train. Wrong house. Wrong
road. He takes his time leaving,
though, even gets out at the pond
and skips a couple of sandstone
flakes across the mirror. There's
something here, isn't there?
This slope, these old erosions—
something that isn't a remnant
of anything, and I bet he feels it too.
Ten years halfway up the cheek
of Roundtop Mountain. To
share this hill's battered light
is to share its purple distances—
those too—I've sensed that much:
a whiff, a twinge, an inkling.

For instance: the phoebes shape
mud cups in which the winter
will lay eggs of ice. For instance:
the fence posts, rotting, stain
the sockets they grow loose in.

Trash Fish; or, Nights Back Home

Something must have spooked them.
  Something got dumped over the guardrail.
    The water under the trestle blurped, convulsed.

It was a good night for a bolt cutter, for hacking something off.
  Someone stashed a fruit jar of gizzards in the trunk.
    Someone limped across the road in front of the tire repair shop.

It was a good night for tying a guitar string to a treble hook.
  A Mustang fish-tailed over gravel, woofers rattling off the bluff.
    Someone took a pull off a fifth, passed it.

It was a good night for climbing the water tower.
  For jumping the fence. A stigma swam upstream.
    Someone pitched a can into the sparks: a good night.

These were the places that demanded, but did not get, a murder.

Ozark Landscape

The face of the owl in the oak snag
lights the remnants of an old plateau.
All across the scarped erosions now
the smell of ice, that moment, atwitch,
astir, when the root reveals a face.
Then the twig becomes a torch,
the crimp of the leaf a hand, a claw.
I'd picked two pebbles from the dry stream bed
and kept them in a moleskin pouch.
To live in the Ozarks is to wait until
the sockets in the bark cry out for eyes.
It is to be ready. Will you set a gourd bowl
brimming shadow at the edge of the coals?
Will you whittle a spoon from a branch?
These are the questions. To live here
is to pluck fur strands from the fence's barb
and save them. It is to turn from the fire
saying *wind is a mallet*, saying *sandstone*.
Will you? Tonight I follow the dents
of tracks to a latch that is a fistful of mud
and I will say—I will—*trust no one.*

The Sign of the Muskellunge

And then the word of the LORD came to me
in the sixth month of my tenth year in that place
saying, "Go down to the river and to that stretch
of water where you have seen the great muskie
stirring clouds of silt with his fins in the shallows."
And though I was surprised to hear from the LORD,
I did as he commanded, and I went through
the pipe gate and the place of stinging nettle;
I walked down the road that ends in water,
and I found a johnboat hidden in a canebrake there.
And I took the boat, which was not mine, and the oars
lying under it, and I journeyed to the shallows
in accordance with the word of the LORD, and behold,
I saw the fish snared in a bankline which I knew belonged
to my neighbor Otha Durrett. Thus said the LORD to me,
"Remove the hook held fast in the fish's jaw,"
and I waded to my knees in the swirling liquid,
but the teeth of the fish bit at me so that I bled.
And the LORD dipped his mighty hand in the grain bin
of light and scattered the glowing seeds across the gravel.
And the LORD said, "Behold, days are coming
when these hills shall no longer be called O´zarks."

And he made the scales of the fish as it swam away
to glitter. He made the heron wading there on stilts
push off from its reflection, and seeing this, I rejoiced
as if the current in its groove might never cease to flow.

Playing the Beer Can

He drinks that one last swallow, flat and warm, swallows
whirling over the pickup's tailgate where he will rest,
as on a dented pew, while the barn's purple shadow dims
to the deeper sigh of fence-line gray. This is the church
of the coyote's track through brambles, of pokeweed,
and of the evening star. These are the last days
of summer, and though he is an old man now, he will play
the pull tab of the can as if it were the plunking of a heart
redeemable still in that aluminum twang of evening
where memories flicker in the rafts of sunlit pollen;
he will play that hollow, clanking tune, there, where he still is—
under the silo's roofless stare, above the river's loosening knot
of mist, and at the edge of an enormous shift of seasons
on a planet whose spinning circuit not only the swallows feel.

It Took Some Doin'

is a way of saying that a task, once finished, was full
   of unexpected toil, that, midway through, it forced you
into doing things you didn't know you could or made
   you redefine the terms or improvise. I'm thinking
of my garden this first clear night of frost, the stars
   shifting suddenly into focus above the mulched
and tucked-in beds. It's fall in the Ozarks, that season
   when I might make the time to drive the back roads
and pull off at some vacant spot where crows drag shadows
   through the woods and I could walk into the trees with them.
It's been a long time, but it would feel right, a deep,
   as if half-remembered, settling in. And I might gather twigs
and light a little rattling fire I'd sit beside as night flowed in
   to fill the steep dissections. I didn't know how to feel
this place, its stone-bound lonesome note of packed
   dirt roads and scorched rock twisted to some ancient
and unreachable ache, its squinting, stingy silence—or
   so it seemed. It took some doin'. Like when our neighbor
backed his brand-new trailer halfway down the mountain,
   through pines, blind curves, and ruts in which long shadows
hid, and onto that sloping shelf where he leveled his new home
   on blocks, one end against the bluff, one hanging into space.

lore

No small area has been studied by folklorists as in-depth and intensely as the Mammoth Cave region.

—*The Harvest and the Reapers: Oral Traditions of Kentucky*

On January 16, 1902, at the base of the bluff known as Dismal Rock, between Bylew and Briar Creeks, the last wolf in Edmonson County, Kentucky, was shot and killed by a local sheep farmer named Noah Duvall. A so-called "outlaw wolf," the large gray male had eluded capture for many months.

biomass: a genealogy

This is the book of the generations of water.
These are the pages, stiff with salts, in which
it came to pass that a sea engendered a vulture,
that a river birthed a lamb, and that a sandbar
begat a shark who swam through brine
and dwelt there for an hundred million years.
These are the books of the two types of stone.
This is the fossil record. And of the offspring
of crinoids and brachiopods: limestone.
And of the children of upthrust and splinter:
an escarpment of flintiest sand. Then out of
the sandstone, a man, bundled in skins, was flung.
And they called his name Noah, and all the days
of the man were twenty-four thousand three hundred six.
And then the wolf, whelped also of water, loped up
through snow that felleth like silt there upon them.
And they gathered them together at the place
of Big Clifty and of Girkin, among tree stumps,
near the hill of the petroglyphs, by the banks
of the creek that floweth through thorns.

q&a

Why does the wolf cock his ear to the wind?
Because the sky at twilight is a mussel shell.

What does he hear?
Note that his guard hairs match the shade between two cedars
   perfectly. Note the galaxy mending a net of stars.

What part does the vulture play?
There are sheep beside the fossil bluffs. Steep pastures and a
   stand of trees.

And the man?
Remember the wind also, ruffling their wool as, in and out of
   shadow, the belled flock clanks and bonks and clunks.

Why is he staring toward that dip in the trees?
Imagine the wolf's bass-throated howl of ferocity and darkness
   and lost hopes. Or, plot the distance between a buffalo trail and
   a road paved with coral.

Why is the road so important?
Because tonight and forever the wolf's howl will remain
   unanswered.

And what of the girl?

She is waiting with a notebook and recorder at the end of many rooms not yet built, down a road that is still a path through leaves.

How will the story end?

She is dreaming of a book about blizzards. She is thinking that the dead are foxfire.

How long now?

She is considering the distance between lit and burnished.

And is that all?

Between quartz and anthracite?

Will she always be this way?

Look at her there. The trees beside the road are almost grown.

lone

That was the end of nights that roamed
in packs—an owl's nest, the hiss of sleet.
When the moth of his breath got stuck
in a web, the wolf freed its wings of dust
and coaxed it—*come now, come*—to a cage
he wove from twigs and hooked the latch.
He rolled two eyes from sap; from ice
he chipped a hull of ribs. And so it was
he forged a self from night's thick pulp.
And so it was he leashed it to the wind.
As he ran, seeds dropped from his fur,
spores flew from the hairs of his tail—
his wake, in time, a slash of trunks, a grid.
That night he slept with curs; snow fell
in loops and twists, the ground by dawn
a slate on which he read the prints of paws,
of hooves, and boots, and then, and then.

dot dot dot

... to this, she adds the shadow of an owl, stars screwed tight
in their sockets...when the man shoulders open the door, it sweeps
a half-moon of boards in the snow...she knows he's been there,
that they've both been there, and she follows them, a century
too late...the line of pebbles where the wolf crosses the creek
each night, he finds one huge paw print frozen in mud...to this,
she adds Orion's Belt...that night he dreams of a shadow,
an unlit edge...she follows the hush, unearthly, of smoke
and drifts...he wakes to something like the sound of a bleat...
the evidence is everywhere: a crinoid stem, the shrapnel
of a shark's teeth lodged in the bluff...water clatters toward him
on hooves made of stone...she subtracts from this one lamb
at the base of the escarpment...wind whets its knife on ice...
she should not go alone...and even the vulture, wobbling
on his raft of air, cannot see that far...but the past comes
with her...even the wolf follows a trail of dots diminishing
to that steep place where seafloor and sandbar collide...

between the wolf and the dog

a freight train splits the difference
between dark and not-yet-light:
inter lupum et canem: enter smoke
in shreds: the wolf sniffs out a glowing
hub of ash: finds the scent of the man
who built the fire: between flame
and smolder: pelage and fur: enter
a night in single digits: enter the outlaw
and a pack of shadows takes him: in:
between fang and tooth: ember and smudge:
exit the galaxy: its nest: oh: enter
that egg: the star that blinds him:

Historical graffito, near Mammoth Dome, Mammoth Cave, Kentucky

Now this hole feller bye the far tuck won two mini pulls
often his licker jug that knight, clumb down oft the heel,
his lags awl warbly, and met, ore sow he claimed,
whole Looser-fur hisself: holler faze, sad he smelt
that suffer, seed them horns and retched fur his gun.
Wall, bout that thyme won of them whole scrunch howls
lat luce, maid ever hare own his had stan up strait.
Hee tern tale an run rat in-two a popular hay was sew scarred.
Hid stair yew inn the aye and knot blank: *he didn't*
caste a shadder, he didn't leaf know tracts hat tall.

eternal, restless

Wind cranks the handle on the grindstone made of ice,
hones one slim evening to a blade of light, then less;
then sparks go skittering among the trees. This is the way
it starts to snow, the way the trails he prowled are lit by ice.
The woman drifts to her window, clicks on a lamp.
Now maybe a gust, off-kilter, gathers up a body of flakes;
maybe it bristles, whimpers, but pretty soon it's scratching
at her door, and pretty soon she's dreaming of the past,
and maybe, just once, his name will cross her mind
like the shadow of an owl. Now even the night begins
to fidget, as if the pulse of rivers in his wrist were beating
to the throb of rivers underground, as if the owl were real,
as if it ever really snowed, or started to, like this.

lupophobia

I.
Ten letters link: a chain, a sobriquet. The man
sleeps under a stone. *Lukos, lupus, argos.*

Now the ridge flakes off its crust and the wolf
lopes up through realms of words: flight,

meaning light and silver. The man's portion:
a name's oiled clamp, but the wolf sheds his fur

and flees, himself a glancing light, then less
and less among black trunks. So what,

from nightmare's edge, comes limping?
What, from out of snow's redactions, veers

and lurches, dragging a metal thorn?

II.
The night is cold
and still. In

the hollow it made
hollow, some-
thing sleeps.
Windless, it is
winter:
something
trembles
in a nest
of shredded
leaves. It
must not be
something,
must not be, be
noticed. Or.
Else: and
still the night
is cold.

wet [weather] spring[s]

he had been given to the forest and forgotten:
a bolt of fur unraveling over the green shadows
of undergrowth; he had taken his place
in the movement of leaves, the unfathomable odor
of black, spiced earth and the oldest wrinkled trunks
and now the trees too were being ransomed;
their roots grasped at rocks and fallen pods.
water in a pool lay hidden in a wooded hollow
under a great cracked bowl of sky and it trembled
in its pebbles to the twang of a saw and the battering
of hooves. everything forgot him and the stars,
flowing on, painted the mossy rocks with light
so pale even a mouse, chased through twigs
by the hunch of her blue shadow, could not be sure.

winter count: a bullet list

- one blew its hollow note across the mouths of caves
- one fled on leather wings
- one swam through currents made of sand
- one chased its tail into a blur
- one dropped its clanging bedload like a stream
- one sputtered into days none thought to name
- one sought the gloom of overhangs
- one stoked the bloodroot's embers into brush
- one knifed the river to the bone
- one lingered in the mind
- one fell behind the herd and did not e'er return

Prehistoric petroglyphs, Dismal Rock bluff shelter

—a hollow sob of wind, nothing more: there came
a dusk when shadows from the flames reared up:
a fork of sticks; there came a line of horned shapes
plunging over tracks and spirals, a night, long ago
but long after, a tin can on the coals' perimeter,
coffee as it boiled and trembled, and the cracked bluff
once again, if only briefly, the silt fan of a river,
the scratches of a fist, the hunter, his shadow by the fire,
as it lurched across incisions, as they dimmed, grain
into stone, that glowing mound he sat beside,
his face in his hands, those little—in the coals—
those little tinkling notes the breeze plucked
when it stirred its fingers through the smoke—

riddle/translation

riddle:

This is the night profound,
A deep that plummet ne'er did sound:
Whose dimness,
And grimness,
And darkness,
And starkness,
And deepness,
And steepness,
And deadness,
And dreadness,
More fitful is made by her lamp's flickering.

translation:

For the wolf abideth in desert places among stones.
He hath tasted the flavors of the wind
and he hath known the company of the talon,
of the cinder, and of the flake.

The sons of men despiseth and scorneth him;
he hath suffered want and hunger
at their hands, but no anger against them shall he kindle.

Yea, though a scorching wind shall be the portion of his meat,
he shall travel like the wings of the owl
and under the shadow of the wings
he shall singeth out for joy.

Selah.

For the moon heareth not his supplications when,
in despair, he crieth out unto it.
For he shall go dumbfounded into shadow.
For he shall passeth out of mind.

Coda

Perhaps in this neglected spot is laid
Some heart once pregnant with celestial fire
　　—Thomas Gray, "Elegy Written in a Country Churchyard"

Old Stith

Surely there was work enough, a lifetime's labor, here
for a practical man, but Old Stith must have wandered away
from all of that: the scythe that needed sharpening,
or the fence that sagged where the deer had jumped it.
Once Charlotte came up from the woods with twelve white pebbles
she discovered in a bois d'arc's knot: Old Stith—who else?
The kind of man who'd dig up cedars and transplant them
in a ring on the farm's highest knob. Sometimes I enter
their mesh of branches now when snow is falling crookedly.
And he must have used a tractor—how else?— to upend
that limestone splinter by the pond and set its base in concrete.
On summer afternoons, the shadow of its finger points across
the water and the little fish swim up into its shade to feed.
What else? Our first spring here, I followed water sliding
down the mountain to where its current hinged off
the bluff and found a tulip poplar rigged with seven
nail-punched buckets to catch the flow as it filtered down
and splattered on a tablet of stone he must have placed there.
What kind of man would dream a water clock like this
or hang a shard of glass on twine to catch the sunlight
beaming through the hayloft's diamond cutout? Old Stith
was dead and gone two years before we came here,
but I like to think he thought of us, that he was tapping out

a message. I lie awake some nights when rain rehearses
the gutter's lines, but soon I'm thinking of his bucket rungs,
that tin unbuttoning tumble as I climb down into the notch
of sleep, of dreams, and find myself—where else?—right here.

notes

Tradition Bearer
"Dumpster Honey" is for John DuVal.
The last line of "Trash Fish; or, Nights Back Home" is adapted from a
   passage in Robert Louis Stevenson's essay "A Gossip on Romance."

lore
I could not have written the poems in "lore" without Barry Lopez's
   magnificent *Of Wolves and Men* as a guide.
"riddle/translation" is adapted from a section of George Lansing Taylor's
   (1835–1903) long poem "In the Maelstrom."

acknowledgments

Grateful acknowledgment is made to the publications in which some of these poems first appeared:

32 Poems: "Old Stith," "Wind in the Ozarks"

American Poetry Review: "q&a," "lone"

Crazyhorse: "Freshwater Drum"

Cumberland River Poetry Review: "eternal, restless," "dot, dot, dot"

The Hampden-Sydney Poetry Review: "[—a hollow sob of wind, nothing more: there came]," "lupophobia," "winter count: a bullet list"

Indiana Review: "First Hard Freeze"

The Journal: "Ozark Landscape"

The Missouri Review: "biomass: a genealogy"

The New Yorker: "Dumpster Honey"

Nimrod: "Not Untwist"

Oxford American: "Of Thorns," "Trundle," "Liquid Assets," "The Hill Itself"

Pleiades: "A Family Story"

Plume: "Road Trip"

The Rumpus: "between the wolf and the dog"

Shenandoah: "Deterred," "Gray Fox, a Resolution of Sorrow"

Smartish Pace: "Trash Fish; or, Nights Back Home"

Subtropics: "The Widder Mercer," "Found Downriver"
Apocalypse Now: Poems and Prose from the End of Days: "First Hard
Freeze," "biomass: a genealogy," "lone," "wet [weather]
spring[s]," "riddle/translation"
The Pushcart Prize XXXVII (2013 anthology): "First Hard Freeze"
Poetry Daily, July 13, 2014: "Freshwater Drum"
Red Holler: An Anthology of Contemporary Appalachian Literature:
"Trash Fish; or, Nights Back Home," "First Hard Freeze," "q&a"

I am grateful to the Arkansas Arts Council, the Walter F.
Laman Public Library, the Porter Fund Literary Prize, the James
E. and Ellen Wadley Roper endowment, and the J. William
Fulbright College of Arts and Sciences at the University of
Arkansas for support during the writing of these poems. Many
thanks to Linda Bierds, Katharine Coles, Hannah New, Stephanie
Warnick, Jessica Booth, Annette Wenda, and everyone at the
University of Utah Press.